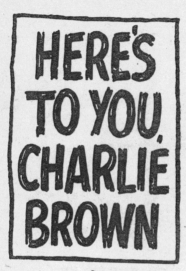

HERE'S TO YOU, CHARLIE BROWN

Selected Cartoons
from YOU CAN'T WIN,
CHARLIE BROWN VOL II

by CHARLES M. SCHULZ

FAWCETT CREST • NEW YORK

HERE'S TO YOU, CHARLIE BROWN

This book, prepared especially for Fawcett Crest Books, a unit of CBS Publications, the Consumer Publishing Division of CBS Inc., comprises the second half of *YOU CAN'T WIN, CHARLIE BROWN*, and is reprinted by arrangement with Holt, Rinehart and Winston, Inc.

ISBN: 0-449-23708-7

Printed in the United States of America

29 28 27 26 25 24 23 22 21 20

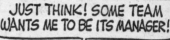

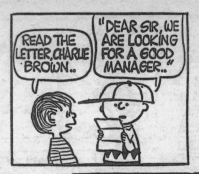

I THINK I'M AHEAD OF MY TIME...

HA! THAT'S A LAUGH! YOU'RE JUST LIKE A LOT OF OTHERS WHO SAY THE SAME THING! IT'S AN EXCUSE! THAT'S WHAT IT IS!

IT'S AN EXCUSE FOR YOUR OWN LACK OF REAL TALENT AND ABILITY!!!

I WAS SUPPOSED TO MEET CHARLIE BROWN HERE AT TWO O'CLOCK, BUT I THINK I'M AHEAD OF MY TIME..

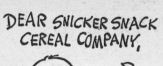

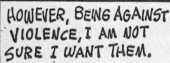

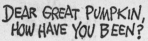

WE ARE LOOKING FORWARD TO YOUR COMING ON HALLOWEEN NIGHT WITH YOUR BAG FULL OF PRESENTS. I HAVE TRIED TO BE A GOOD BOY ALL YEAR.

HAVE YOU NOTICED?

...AND THEN, SALLY, ON HALLOWEEN NIGHT, THE GREAT PUMPKIN APPEARS!

HE FLIES THROUGH THE AIR, AND BRINGS TOYS TO ALL THE CHILDREN OF THE WORLD!

HA!

I DON'T THINK SHE BELIEVED ME...

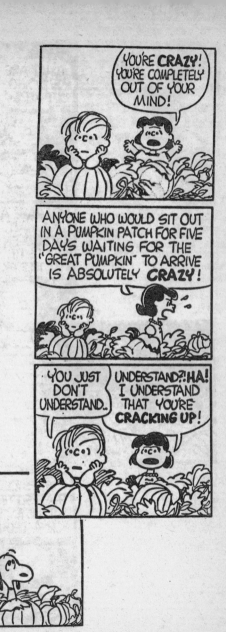

EACH YEAR THE "GREAT PUMPKIN" RISES OUT OF THE PUMPKIN PATCH THAT HE THINKS IS THE MOST SINCERE

HE'S GOT TO PICK THIS ONE! HE'S GOT TO! I DON'T SEE HOW A PUMPKIN PATCH CAN BE MORE SINCERE THAN THIS ONE!

YOU CAN LOOK ALL AROUND AND THERE'S NOT A SIGN OF HYPOCRISY...

NOTHING BUT SINCERITY AS FAR AS THE EYE CAN SEE!

ISN'T LINUS GOING OUT FOR "TRICKS OR TREATS"?

NO, HE'S SITTING IN THE PUMPKIN PATCH WAITING FOR THE GREAT PUMPKIN TO APPEAR

WELL, WHEN YOU GO UP TO THIS NEXT HOUSE, ASK THE LADY FOR AN EXTRA TREAT FOR YOUR LITTLE BROTHER WHO IS SITTING OUT IN THE PUMPKIN PATCH

ALL I GOT FROM HER WAS A VERY PECULIAR LOOK!

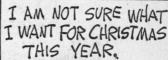

DEAR SANTA CLAUS,
HOW HAVE YOU BEEN?
HOW IS YOUR WIFE?

I AM NOT SURE WHAT
I WANT FOR CHRISTMAS
THIS YEAR.

SOMETIMES IT IS VERY
HARD TO DECIDE.

PERHAPS YOU SHOULD
SEND ME YOUR CATALOGUE.

ONE LAST FLING!

SHE LOVES ME...SHE LOVES ME NOT...

SHE LOVES ME...SHE LOVES ME NOT...SHE..

IT IS DIFFICULT FOR ME TO BELIEVE THAT A FLOWER HAS THE GIFT OF PROPHECY!

MY HOME IS ALWAYS OPEN TO THOSE WHO ENJOY DISCUSSION GROUPS!

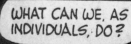

DO YOU THINK CHARLIE BROWN REALLY COULD GET NOMINATED FOR PRESIDENT?

WHAT DO YOU MEAN, NOMINATED? DON'T YOU KNOW **ANYTHING**?

FIRST YOU HAVE-TO BECOME A **PRINCE**.... **THEN** YOU GET TO BE PRESIDENT!!

IT'S FRIGHTENING WHEN I REALIZE HOW LITTLE I REALLY KNOW ABOUT GOVERNMENTAL AFFAIRS!

IF YOU THINK THOSE ARE FUNNY FACES YOU'RE MAKING, THEN YOU'RE SADLY MISTAKEN!

NOBODY APPRECIATES GOOD HUMOR ANY MORE

I CAN'T REMEMBER EVER HAVING A THEORY EXPLODED QUITE SO FAST!

..AND SO THE OPHTHALMOLOGIST SAID I HAVE TO START WEARING GLASSES...

AT FIRST I WAS PRETTY UPSET... IT WAS A REAL EMOTIONAL BLOW... ALL SORTS OF THINGS WENT THROUGH MY MIND...

BUT, FINALLY, ONE THOUGHT SEEMED TO STAND OUT..

WHAT WAS THAT?

IT'S KIND OF NICE TO BE ABLE TO SEE WHAT'S GOING ON!

NOT AGAIN?

YES, AND I CAN'T FIND THEM ANYWHERE!

WELL, IF YOU'RE GOING TO WEAR GLASSES, YOU'RE GOING TO HAVE TO LEARN TO HANG ON TO THEM!

"GENTLEMEN, I'D LIKE TO PRESENT TO YOU THE NEW CHAIRMAN OF THE BOARD!"

GOOD GRIEF! DON'T YOU HAVE ANY PATIENCE AT ALL?!!

THE SNICKER SNACK CEREAL COMPANY SPENT FORTY THOUSAND DOLLARS TO DEVELOP A BOX TOP THAT CAN BE OPENED EASILY, AND YOU RIP THE WHOLE TOP CLEAN OFF!!

MY HEART BLEEDS FOR THE SNICKER SNACK COMPANY!

ZOOM

WITH A LITTLE PRACTICE
I BET I COULD GET THE
SHOES, TOO!

NOBODY LIKES ME!

I WISH I COULD LIKE YOU, CHARLIE BROWN, BUT I CAN'T...

IF I WERE TO LIKE YOU, IT WOULD BE ADMITTING THAT I WAS LOWERING MY STANDARDS! YOU WOULDN'T WANT ME TO DO THAT, WOULD YOU? BE REASONABLE!

I HAVE STANDARDS THAT I HAVE SET UP FOR LIKING PEOPLE, AND YOU JUST DON'T MEET THOSE STANDARDS! IT WOULDN'T BE REASONABLE FOR ME TO LIKE YOU!

I HATE MYSELF FOR BEING SO UNREASONABLE!

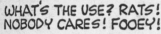

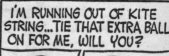

HAPPINESS IS FEELING THE WIND AND THE RAIN IN YOUR HAIR!

SORT OF!